Planets in Our Solar System

# MARS

by Jody S. Rake

a Capstone company — publishers for children

Raintree is an imprint of Capstone Global Library Limited, a company incorporated in England and Wales having its registered office at 264 Banbury Road, Oxford, OX2 7DY – Registered company number: 6695582

www.raintree.co.uk
myorders@raintree.co.uk



Edited by Alison Deering
Designed by Jennifer Bergstrom
Original illustrations © Capstone Global Library Limited 2021
Picture research by Tracy Cummins
Production by Tori Abraham
Originated by Capstone Global Library Ltd

978 1 3982 0519 2 (hardback)
978 1 3982 0520 8 (paperback)

**British Library Cataloguing in Publication Data**
A full catalogue record for this book is available from the British Library.

**Acknowledgements**
We would like to thank the following for permission to reproduce photographs: Alamy: Art Directors & TRIP, 8; NASA: Hubble Site/Illustration: James Gitlin (STScI), 17, JPL, 22, JPL/Cornell, 16, JPL/Texas A&M/Cornell, 14, JPL/USGS, 18, 19, JPL-Caltech, 23, 27, JPL-Caltech/Cornell/Arizona State Univ, 13, JPL-Caltech/University of Arizona, 15; Science Source: BABAK A. TAFRESHI, 5, 28, SCIENCE PHOTO LIBRARY, 11; Shutterstock: Alones, 1, 26 right, Aphelleon, Cover, Christos Georghiou, 6, Dotted Yeti, Cover left, Elena11, 20, Johan Swanepoel, 25, khak, 10, Luca Fabbri, 9, Nerthuz, Back Cover, Timothy Hodgkinson, 26 left, Tristan3D, 7, Vadim Sadovski, 21; Wikipedia: NASA, 12. **Design elements:** Shutterstock: Arcady, BLACKDAY, ebes, LynxVector, phipatbig, Stefan Holm, veronchick_84



Printed and bound in India

# Contents



Words in **bold** are in the glossary.

# The red planet

The night sky is full of lights. One light looks pink, not white. It is not a star. It is the planet Mars. Mars is one of the planets closest to Earth.

Mars is covered with red dust. It is lit up by the Sun. From Earth, Mars looks like a small pink light.

**From Earth, Mars looks like a pink star.**

Mars

**The orbits of the planets in our solar system**

Mars is the fourth planet from the Sun. It moves in a path around the Sun. This path is called an **orbit**.

This path is not a perfect circle. It is shaped like an egg. That means some days Mars is a bit closer to the Sun. Some days it is a bit further away.

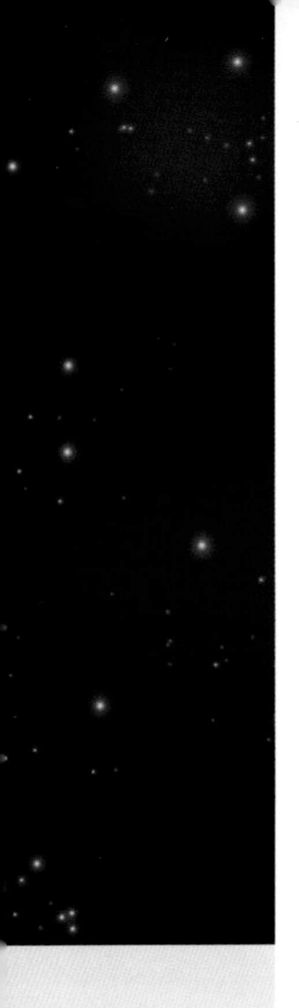

Mars zooms around the Sun very quickly. It travels more than 1.6 million km (1 million miles) in one Earth day!

Mars is about half the size of Earth. Imagine Earth was the size of a cherry tomato. Mars would be as big as a blueberry.

**Mars is roughly half the size of Earth.**

## Close but so far

People have known about Mars for thousands of years. A **scientist** was the first person to see it. His name was Galileo.

He used a tool called a **telescope**. He studied Mars more than 400 years ago.

The scientist Galileo

A statue of Mars, the Roman god of war

Mars was named after the Roman god of war. The planet's red colour made people think of war and fighting. Its moons are named after the war god's sons.

**Mars is far away from the Sun and Earth.**

Mars is millions of kilometres from Earth. Sometimes we can see it in the sky at night.

Mars and Earth circle the Sun at different speeds. Sometimes the two planets are on the same side of the Sun. Then they are closest together.

Sometimes they are on opposite sides of the Sun. Then they are more than seven times further apart.

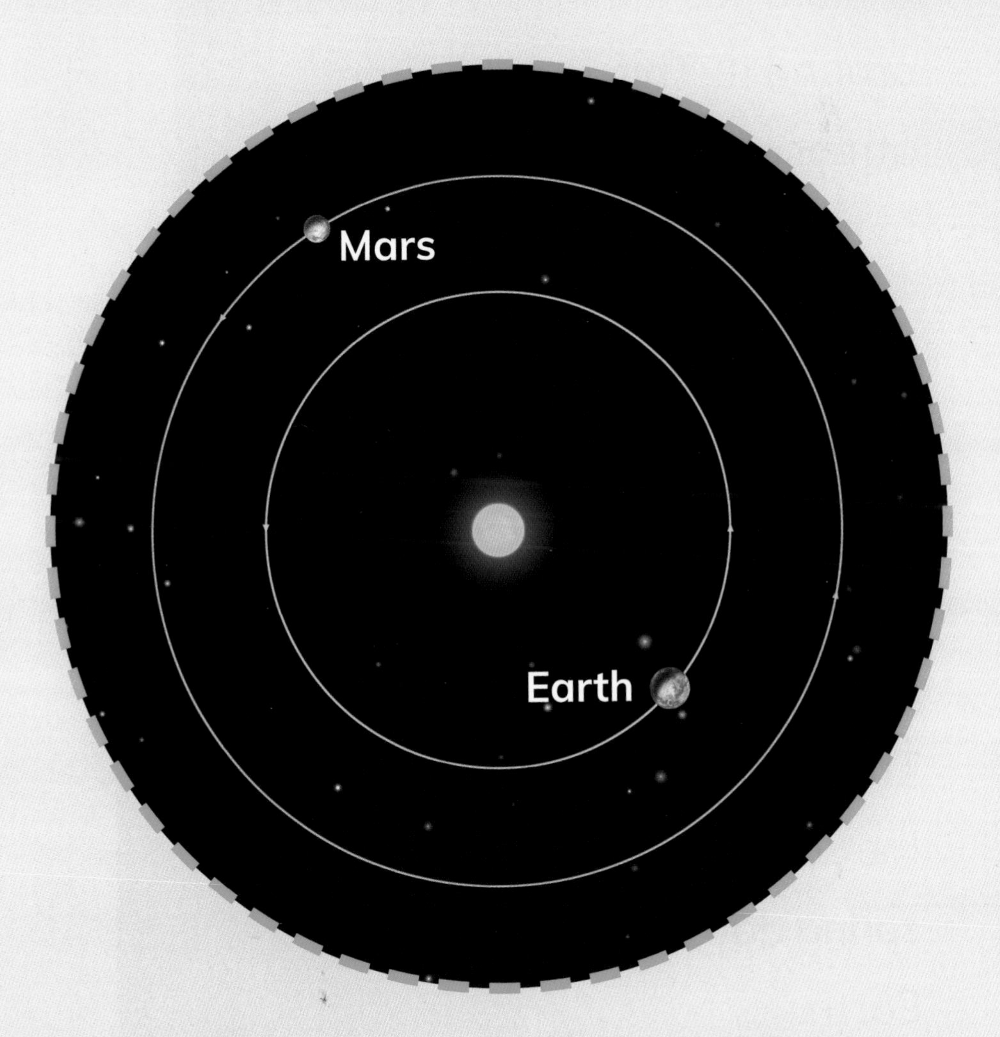


Mars and Earth circle the Sun at different speeds.

# Too cold!

Mars has a thin layer of gases around it. This is called the atmosphere. There is no air to breathe.

Mars does not get very hot. The warmest it gets is 20 degrees Celsius (70 degrees Fahrenheit). This is about the same as a spring day on Earth.

A layer of gases surrounds Mars

Late afternoon on Mars

Mars gets very cold at night. The temperature drops far below freezing. This is because the Sun's heat disappears.

**Sunset on Mars makes the planet very cold.**

**Frost on the surface of Mars**

The ground on Mars is the warmest place to be. It gets colder only a metre or so up. If you could stand on Mars, it would feel like spring at your feet. But at your head, it would feel like winter!

## Rocky landscape

Mars is a rocky planet. Rocks with **rusty** metals give the planet its red colour.

If you were standing on Mars, you would see more colours. The planet also looks brown and gold.

**Mars is red and rocky.**

**Dust storms on Mars can last for months.**

Winds on Mars cause giant dust storms. Clouds of red dust cover much of the planet. It can take months for the dust to settle.

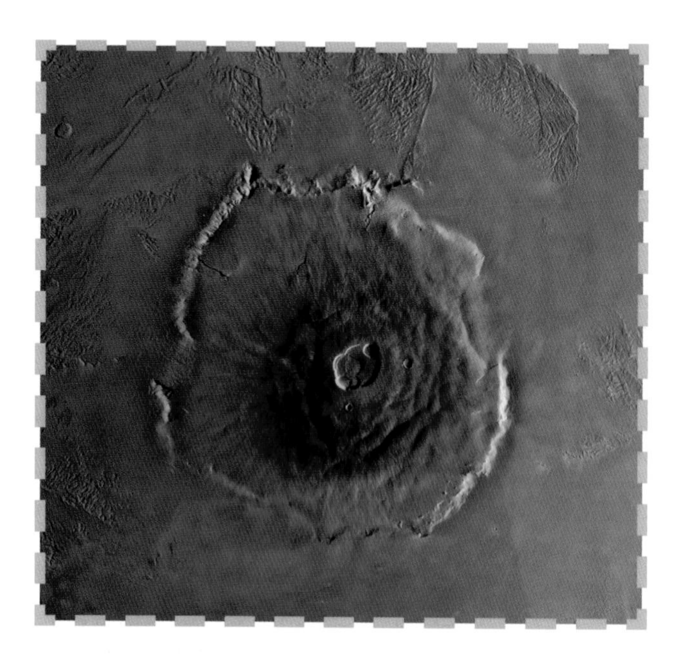

**Olympus Mons, the tallest mountain on Mars, seen from above**

Scientists think Mars used to be covered with water. Now it only has a little water. Most of it is frozen. Some of it is underground. It is very salty.

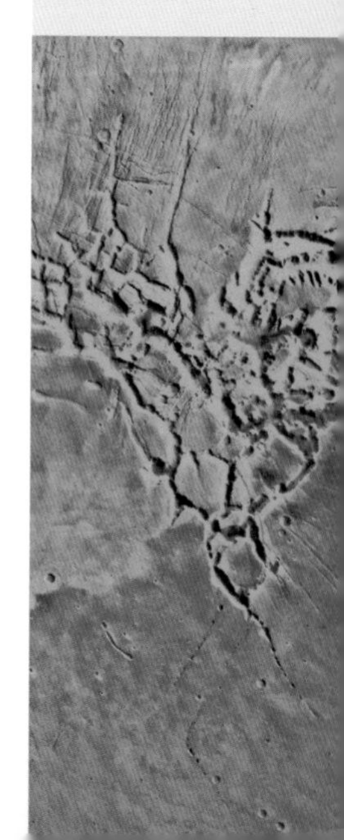

Mars has many mountains. The tallest mountain is called Olympus Mons. It is nearly three times taller than Earth's tallest mountain.

Mars also has large, deep valleys called canyons. The biggest one is about ten times longer than the Grand Canyon. That is about four times longer than the length of Britain!

The deepest canyon on Mars

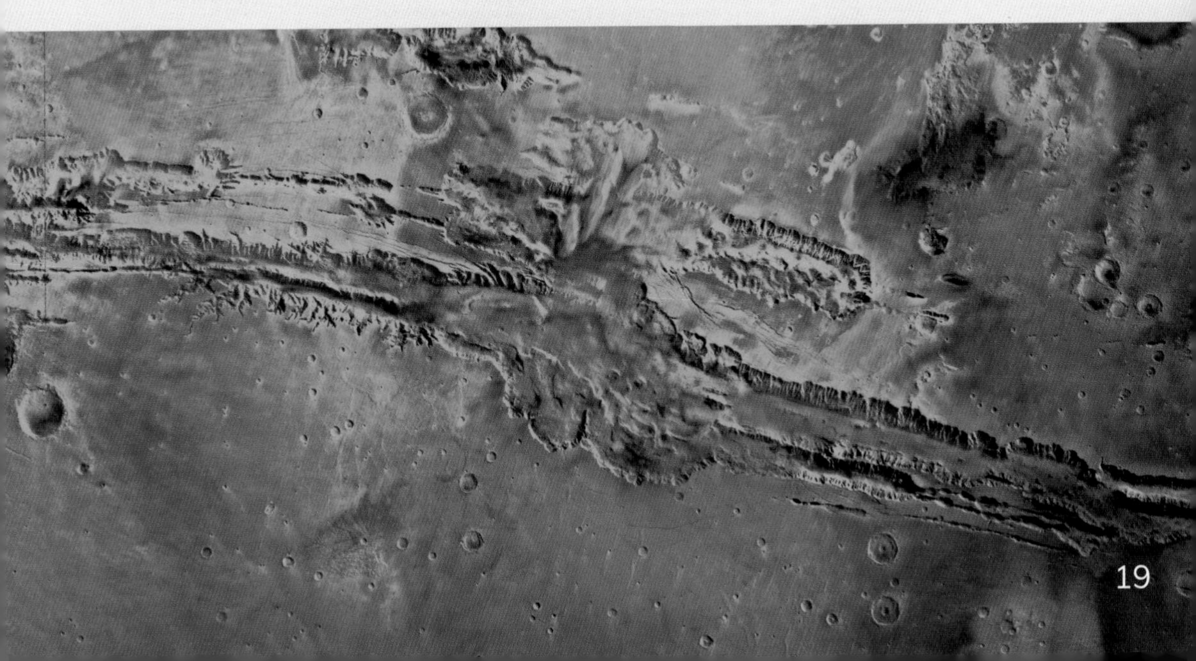

**Mars and its two cratered moons**

Two small moons circle Mars. We first learned about them about 150 years ago.

The first moon is called Phobos. It circles closer to Mars. It moves very quickly. It circles the planet three times a day.

Phobos

This moon is covered with holes. These are called craters. The biggest one covers almost half the moon.

The second moon is Deimos. It circles further away. It takes 30 hours to circle Mars. It is smaller and smoother looking.

**Deimos** **Phobos**

# Wheeled explorers of Mars

Many spacecraft have gone to explore Mars. Satellites flew past more than 50 years ago. They took pictures.

A satellite circles Mars.

About 25 years ago, a small vehicle called a **rover** landed on Mars. It had wheels to drive. It also had parts used to explore. Since then, several rovers have landed on Mars.

Three types of Mars rovers

No people have travelled to Mars yet. People hope to visit there one day. The trip would take six to nine months in a fast spacecraft.

# Could we live on Mars?

Mars spins, just like other planets. It takes about 25 hours to spin once. That means one day on Mars is only a bit longer than a day on Earth.

One year on Mars is 687 days on Earth. A year there is almost twice as long as a year on Earth. Imagine having your birthday every other year!

One trip around the Sun equals one year on any planet.

Gravity is stronger on Earth than on Mars.

**Gravity** is the force that holds us on the ground. Gravity on Earth is three times stronger than it is on Mars. Imagine you weigh 45 kilograms (100 pounds) on Earth. You would only weigh 17 kg (38 pounds) on Mars.

There could not be life as we know it on Mars. There is no air. There is no water to drink. It gets too cold on Mars. Scientists are studying Mars to see if it ever had life.

**Scientists are very curious about Mars.**

Mars comes closest to Earth about once every two years. It looks like a pink star. But Mars doesn't twinkle.

People have been interested in the red planet for hundreds of years. One day, people may be able to visit Mars!

People on Earth study the night sky.

# Fast facts

**Name:**
Mars

**Location:**
4th planet from the Sun

**Planet type:**
rocky

**Discovered:**
first seen through a telescope in 1609

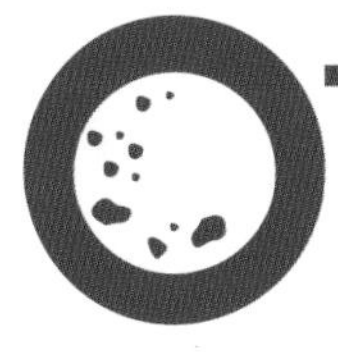

**Moons:**
2 – Phobos and Deimos

# Glossary

**atmosphere** layer of gases that surrounds some planets, dwarf planets and moons

**crater** hole made when large pieces of rock crash into a planet or moon's surface

**gas** something that is not solid or liquid and does not have a definite shape

**gravity** force that pulls objects together

**orbit** travel around an object in space; an orbit is also the path an object follows when circling an object in space

**rover** small vehicle that people can move by using remote control; rovers are used to explore objects in space

**rusty** covered with a reddish-brown crust

**satellite** spacecraft used to send signals and information from one place to another

**scientist** person who studies the world around us

**telescope** tool people use to look up at objects in space; telescopes make objects in space look closer than they really are

# Find out more

## Books

*Journey to Mars* (Super Space Science), David Hawksett (Raintree, 2019)

*Mars: Explore the mysteries of the Red Planet*, DK (DK Children, 2020)

*Space* (Explorer Tales), Nick Hunter (Raintree, 2013)

## Websites

**www.bbc.co.uk/bitesize/topics/zdrrd2p/articles/ztsdj6f**
Learn more about the rocky planets.

**www.dkfindout.com/uk/space**
Find out more about space, including all the planets in our solar system.

**www.esa.int/kids/en/home**
Learn more about space exploration from the European Space Agency.

# Index